A-Zo.
Key Concepts in Primary Mathematics

Claire Mooney

LearningMatters

First published in 2003 by Learning Matters Ltd.

British Library Cataloguing in Publication Data
A CIP record for this book is available from the British Library.

ISBN 1 903300 48 7

Cover design by Topics — The Creative Partnership
Text design by Code 5 Design Associates Ltd
Project management by Deer Park Productions
Typeset by PDQ Typesetting
Printed and bound in Great Britain by Bell & Bain Ltd, Glasgow

Learning Matters Ltd
33 Southernhay East
Exeter EX1 1NX
01392 215560
info@learningmatters.co.uk
www.learningmatters.co.uk

Contents

Introduction

This *A–Z of Key Concepts in Primary Mathematics* has been written as a reference guide to many of the mathematical concepts that you will be required to teach within a primary classroom. The list is by no means exhaustive but does include most of the areas you will encounter. It is designed to be easily accessible and to offer support to you as you refresh and develop your mathematical subject knowledge.

The mathematical knowledge required to teach effectively can be thought of as mathematical subject knowledge combined with pedagogical knowledge. When combined these two forms of knowledge ensure teachers can choose appropriate examples, analogies and representations to support the mathematical learning of children. Both these areas are given in-depth coverage in the *Achieving QTS* series (Mooney et al., 2002a, 2002b; Mooney and Fletcher, 2003).

A sound personal understanding of mathematics is a critical factor in the complex process of teaching mathematics. It will support you in:

- planning mathematics and numeracy lessons and sequences of lessons;
- setting challenging teaching and learning objectives;
- preparing appropriate, motivating mathematics resources;
- evaluating the progress in children's mathematics learning;
- supporting mathematically low-attaining children;
- extending mathematically high-attaining children;
- identifying and remediating children's mathematical errors and misconceptions;
- asking and answering appropriate mathematical questions in class to support and extend children's learning.

As well as purely mathematical concepts this book also includes references to some of the people who have contributed to mathematics throughout history. This helps to contextualise some areas of mathematics. It also introduces you to some of the people who felt so passionately about the subject that they even died for mathematics!

The *A–Z of Key Concepts in Primary Mathematics* has been written for:

- trainee teachers working towards meeting the requirements of the Professional Standards;

- teachers in their induction year working towards meeting the Induction Standards;
- teacher mentors working with trainees during periods of school-based training;
- experienced teachers as an easily accessible reference text;
- teaching assistants supporting children in group and individual work.

The book is organised with straightforward alphabetical entries that are, when appropriate, cross-referenced to other items to help you make connections between key concepts. A margin icon like this ☿ and bold type has been used to highlight cross-references.

The content of this book has been designed to support the development of mathematical vocabulary as suggested by the National Numeracy Strategy. It does not attempt to cover every word and phrase identified within the strategy's *Mathematical Vocabulary* book but does address all the strands. It also includes a wider range of topics designed to ensure you have an understanding of mathematics that far exceeds that of the children you are teaching. This will ensure you can extend them appropriately, having a good understanding of the areas/ concepts they will be studying as they progress throughout their schooling.

This book has been written in the hope that it helps support and develop your mathematics subject knowledge, and also in the hope that it introduces you to some of the history and passion associated with the subject. Although for some of the people outlined in this book mathematics had some quite alarming consequences, I'm sure you will find that, generally, it doesn't damage your health too severely! Enjoy it!

Claire Mooney
May 2003

A–Z of Key Concepts

abscissa
The first number in a pair of Cartesian co-ordinates. The abscissa always represents the distance along the x-axis (the horizontal axis).

abstract number
(See also **concrete number**.)
A number on its own without reference to any particular object or set of elements.

acute angle
An angle that is less than 90°:

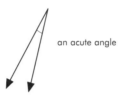

an acute angle

add/addition
An operation that combines two or more numbers, the addends, to form a single number, the sum. The symbol for addition is +.

addend
One of a set of numbers that is to be added. For example, in 2 + 3 = 5, both 2 and 3 are the addends.

algebra
This deals with the study of mathematical structure, the representation of patterns and relationships, and using letters or other symbols to stand for quantities. (See also **al-Khwarizmi, Muhammad**.)

algorithm
A systematic method of computation named after Muhammad al-Khwarizmi.

al-Khwarizmi, Muhammad (c. 780–c. 850)
An Arab mathematician who wrote a book entitled *Hisab al-jabr wa'l muqabalah*. This translates as *Calculation by Restoration and Reduction*. His ideas have been so influential in the world of mathematics that the word *al-jabr* in the title of his book has become the algebra of today.

angle

A measurement of turn (see also **acute, obtuse, reflex, right** and **straight angles**; also **complementary** and **supplementary angles**). Units of measure: degrees (°). There are 360° in a full turn.

anti-clockwise

In the opposite direction to the way the hands of a clock travel:

anti-clockwise

approximately equal to

There are times when calculating or solving mathematical problems that the answer achieved can only be an approximation and not an accurate answer. This is frequently the case when dealing with most aspects of measurement. Any measure that is taken can only be the nearest approximation, depending upon the accuracy of the measuring instrument used. Calculations using π are only ever approximations as π is an irrational number and therefore the exact value is not known.

arc

A section of a curve. It may form part of the circumference of a circle.

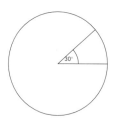

To find the arc of this circle we use the fact that we know the angle is 30° and that there are 360° in the full circle. This gives the arc as a fraction of the whole circumference (i.e. 30/360°). If the circumference is multiplied by this fraction, the answer is equal to the length of the arc.

$$\text{Length of the arc} = \frac{30}{360} \times 2\pi r$$
$$= \frac{\pi r}{6}$$

Archimedean solids

These were first described by Archimedes – hence the name. Each face of an Archimedean solid is a regular polygon. Unlike the Platonic solids, where each face is an identical regular polygon, two or more different regular polygons appear in each Archimedean solid. Around each vertex of the solid the same polygons appear in the same order – for example, triangle–square–triangle–square in the cuboctahedron:

There are 13 Archimedean solids: (the numbers shown in brackets indicate the polygons which surround each of the vertices of the solid. For example, (3, 4, 3, 4) describes the triangle–square–triangle–square of the cuboctahedron):

(3, 4, 3, 4)	cuboctahedron
(3, 5, 3, 5)	icosidodecahedron
(3, 6, 6)	truncated tetrahedron
(4, 6, 6)	truncated octahedron
(3, 8, 8)	truncated cube
(5, 6, 6)	truncated icosahedron
(3, 10, 10)	truncated dodecahedron
(3, 4, 4, 4)	rhombicuboctahedron, sometimes called the *small rhombicuboctahedron*
(4, 6, 8)	truncated cuboctahedron, sometimes called the *great rhombicuboctahedron*
(3, 4, 5, 4)	rhombicosidodecahedron, sometimes called the *small rhombicosidodecahedron*
(4, 6, 10)	truncated icosidodecahedron, sometimes called the *great rhombicosidodecahedron*
(3, 3, 3, 3, 4)	snub cube, also called the *snub cuboctahedron*
(3, 3, 3, 3, 5)	snub dodecahedron, also called the *snub icosidodecahedron*

Archimedes (287–212 BCE)

As well as identifying the Archimedean solids, Archimedes found proofs for finding the areas and volumes of circles, spheres, conics, spirals, curves and surfaces. He also began the science of calculus. As with other early mathematicians it is the story surrounding his death that many people find interesting. Archimedes had spent his life in Syracuse, happily studying mathematics when, in his late seventies, the area was invaded by the Roman army. The story recounts that, during the invasion, Archimedes was so engrossed studying a geometric figure in the sand that he failed to notice and respond to a Roman soldier's questions. As a result he was speared to death.

area

Area is the size of the surface. It is measured in square units. It is sometimes easier to use a formula to calculate the area of certain shapes.

Aristotle (384–322 BCE)
A Greek philosopher who laid the foundations for many branches of science known today. He is also remembered for arguing that the number zero should be outlawed because it disrupted the consistency of the other numbers!

arithmetic
This is the part of mathematics that is concerned with the properties of numbers and the four rules of numbers (also called number operations).

array
An arrangement in rows and columns. For example:

```
•  •  •  •  •  •
•  •  •  •  •  •
•  •  •  •  •  •
```

ascending order
Increasing in size. For example, if the numbers 2, 5, 1, 7, 9, 3 were written in ascending order they would read 1, 2, 3, 5, 7, 9.

Aspasia (470–410 BCE)
Born in Miletos in Ionia, Aspasia was well educated woman who moved to Athens to support her intellectual development further. In 445 BCE she became mistress to Pericles, the military and political leader. She was a very celebrated teacher and, indeed, appears in Plato's *Dialogues* as a teacher of Socrates. Although not necessarily a true mathematician, her use of logic and deductive reasoning helped to foster the climate in which mathematics developed and flourished.

associative law
This is the property by which numbers can be regrouped to simplify a question while making no difference to the answer. It is true for addition and multiplication:

$$(a + b) + c = a + (b + c) \qquad (a \times b) \times c = a \times (b \times c)$$

It is written generally as:

$$(a * b) * c = a * (b * c)$$

average
The general term used when employing one number to represent a set of data. (See also **mean**, **median** and **mode**.)

axis
(Plural, axes.) These are lines used to locate points on graphs. The vertical number line is called the y-axis and the horizontal

number line is called the x-axis. The point where the two axes intersect is called the origin. Cartesian co-ordinates use the distance along the x-axis and the distance along the y-axis to locate a point.

axis of symmetry

This is the line about which a shape can be folded so that one half sits exactly on top of the other half. If a shape has an axis of symmetry it is said to have reflective symmetry:

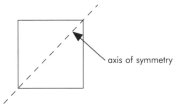

axis of symmetry

Babylonian number system

A number system used by the ancient Babylonian civilisation. In 2000 BCE they were using a place value system but did not have a symbol to stand for zero. They used a base-60 system (sexagesimal system) which is still the basis for our measurement systems related to time and angular measurement:

1	𒁹	11	𒌋𒁹
2	𒈫	12	𒌋𒈫
3	𒐈	20	𒎙
4	𒃻	21	𒎙𒁹
5	𒐊	22	𒎙𒈫
6	𒐋	30	𒀹
7	𒐌	31	𒀹𒁹
8	𒐍	40	𒑖
9	𒐎	50	𒑙
10	𒌋	59	𒑙𒐎

bar chart

A graph that uses bars to represent discrete data. The length of each bar represents the number of items (the frequency), and the tallest bar represents the data that occurs most often (the mode). Each bar is separate to show that the data is discrete.

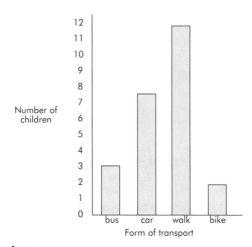

What is the most popular form of transport?

bar line chart

A graph that uses lines to represent data in the same way as a bar chart.

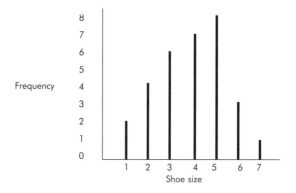

base

1. Index form   In index form, the base is the number that is used with an exponent or index to represent multiplication of a number by itself in a concise way. For example:

7 is the *index*

2 is the *base* → $2^7 = 128$

2. Place value   The Hindu–Arabic place value number system that we use is a base-10 system. Each column can contain any of the ten digits from 0 to 9. The column headings are constructed from powers of 10 (the base):

Thousands	Hundreds	Tens	Units
$10 \times 10 \times 10$	10×10	10	1
10^3	10^2	10^1	10^0

In the same way it is possible to use different number bases to represent place value systems. For example (base 3):

81	27	9	3	1
$3 \times 3 \times 3 \times 3$	$3 \times 3 \times 3$	3×3	3	1
3^4	3^3	3^2	3^1	3^0

(See also **binary**.)

3. Shape   In considering the set of pyramids in 3-D shape, it is possible to name them as systematically as any other polyhedra based on the number of faces they have. However, each pyramid can also take its name from the shape of its base. For example:

This pyramid can be called a pentahedron as it has 5 faces. It can also be called a square pyramid, taking its name from the shape of its base. This is also true for the set of prisms.

between

This implies an interval which does not include the first and last elements – for example, the set of whole numbers between 2 and 9 is 3, 4, 5, 6, 7, 8.

binary

A base-2 counting system. Because it is base 2, it uses only two digits 0 and 1. The column headings in base 2 are units, twos, fours, eights, sixteens, thirty-twos, etc. Numbers from 1 to 20 would be written as follows:

16	8	4	2	U		Base 10
				1		1
			1	0		2
			1	1		3
		1	0	0		4
		1	0	1		5
		1	1	0		6
		1	1	1		7
	1	0	0	0		8

```
1 0 0 1        9
1 0 1 0       10
1 0 1 1       11
1 1 0 0       12
1 1 0 1       13
1 1 1 0       14
1 1 1 1       15
1 0 0 0 0       16
1 0 0 0 1       17
1 0 0 1 0       18
1 0 0 1 1       19
1 0 1 0 0       20
```

(See also **base**.)

bisect

To divide into two equal parts:

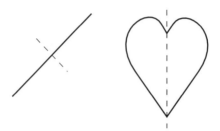

block graph

A graph used to display discrete data where blocks are used to represent items. Block graphs do not require a side scale as the blocks can easily be counted – as such they should only be used when the frequencies are not too large:

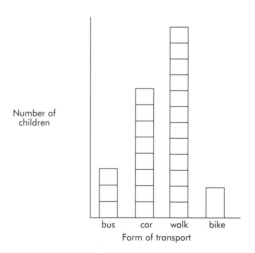

What is the most popular form of transport?

Number of children

bus   car   walk   bike

Form of transport

BODMAS

The order of precedence given to the operations when working out complex expressions. It stands for:

B – brackets
O – of (or other)
D – division
M – multiplication
A – addition
S – subtraction

For example:

$10 \div 2 + 8 \times 3 - \frac{1}{2}$ of $6 + (4 - 2)$	Brackets
$10 \div 2 + 8 \times 3 - \frac{1}{2}$ of $6 + 2$	Of
$10 \div 2 + 8 \times 3 - 3 + 2$	Division
$5 + 8 \times 3 - 3 + 2$	Multiplication
$5 + 24 - 3 + 2$	Addition
$31 - 3$	Subtraction
28	

box and whisker plot

A graph that allows for distributions to be represented graphically. For example, when considering the range of distribution of shoe sizes in a Year 6 class:

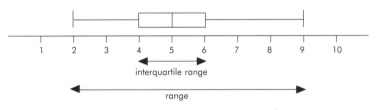

This box and whisker plot shows that the middle 50% of the class (the interquartile range) have shoe sizes between size 4 and 6. Each of the whiskers represents the upper and lower 25%. The line through the box indicates the median shoe size is 5.

Brahe, Tycho (1546–1601)

A Scandinavian mathematician and astronomer. Prior to the invention of the telescope he collected the largest and most accurate set of astronomical facts. Johannes Kepler continued with his work on planetary motion. It is said that he lost the tip of his nose in a duel over a geometry problem!

calculate

To use the operations of addition, subtraction, multiplication and division to work out an answer.

cancel

Dividing both the top and bottom number of a fraction (the numerator and the denominator) by the same number to create an equivalent fraction. For example:

$$\frac{2}{10} = \frac{1}{5} \text{ (dividing the top and bottom by 2)}$$

capacity

How much liquid volume a container can hold when full. Units – metric: millilitre, decilitre, litre; imperial: pint, quart, gallon.

cardinality

The cardinal aspect of number means using a number to describe how many there are in a set. For example:

 5 bears

Carroll diagram

A diagram devised by Lewis Carroll (real name Charles Dodgson) of Alice fame! It is used to consider if something has, or does not have, two different properties. For example:

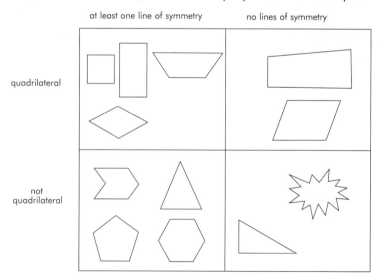

Cartesian coordinates

A pair of numbers that locate a point on a plane with reference to two axes (can also refer to three axes in order to locate a point in three dimensions). In Cartesian co-ordinates the x-axis

(horizontal axis) is always written first (see also **abscissa,
ordinate, x-axis** and **y-axis**.) Cartesian co-ordinates are
named after the French philosopher and scientist René
Descartes (1596–1650):

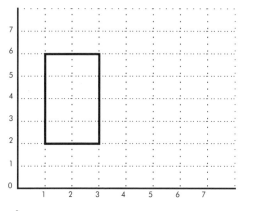

the rectangle drawn
here has the following
co-ordinates:

(1, 2)
(3, 2)
(3, 6)
(1, 6)

chance
(See **probability**.)

Chinese
Since 400 BCE or even earlier the Chinese have used a decimal
place-value system. Although they now use the Hindu-Arabic
script for many things, they still use their own number script as
well. In addition to the symbol for zero as shown below, the
Chinese also use 0:

	0	1	2	3	4	5	6	7	8	9	10	100	1000	10000
traditional Chinese	零	一	二	三	四	五	六	七	八	九	十	百	千	萬

Number names are far more consistent than our own. After ten
comes eleven, which is 'ten one', twelve is 'ten two' and so on.
Twenty is 'two ten', twenty-one is 'two ten one' and so on.

chord
Divides a circle into two segments:

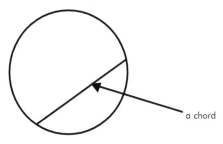

a chord

'chunking'

An informal name to describe an informal method of division using repeated subtraction. For example, $7320 \div 60$:

$$
\begin{array}{ll}
7320 & \\
-\ \underline{6000} & (100 \times 60) \\
1320 & \\
-\ \underline{1200} & (20 \times 60) \\
120 & \\
-\ \underline{120} & (2 \times 60)
\end{array}
$$

(Answer: $7320 \div 60 = 122$. This is found by adding up the number of 60s in the right-hand column (i.e. the numbers before the multiplication sign).

circle

A closed curve with an infinite number of lines of symmetry. It is the set of all points a fixed distance from a fixed point on a plane (i.e. the centre of the circle). A circle is not a polygon (a circle has no knees!). Calculating the areas and circumferences of circles involves the use of the irrational number π. As π is irrational it means the number of decimal places is infinite. The fact that we use an estimation for π in calculations implies that any measure of area or circumference is only an approximation!

One of the simplest ways to show how to calculate the area of a circle is shown below. First you have to imagine the circle cut into lots of sectors. Next you have to rearrange them as shown below. Now imagine the sectors becoming smaller and smaller. As this happens the shape they are forming when rearranged becomes closer and closer to a rectangle. But what are the dimensions of the rectangle? It is quite easy to see that the width of the rectangle is equal to the radius of the circle, and the length is also quite straightforward. As half the sectors are placed facing one direction and the other half are facing the opposite direction, to make the opposite sides of the rectangle, it can be seen that the length is equal to half the circumference:

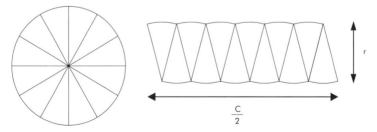

In order to calculate the area of the circle we simply need to calculate the area of the corresponding rectangle of which we know the dimensions:

$$\text{Area of the rectangle} = \text{length} \times \text{breadth}$$
$$= \frac{C}{2} \times r$$

We already know that $C = 2\pi r$ so substituting gives:

$$\text{Area} = \frac{2\pi r}{2} \times r$$
$$= \pi r \times r$$
$$= \pi r^2$$

circumference

The distance around a circle. It can be calculated using the fact that π is obtained by dividing the circumference (C) of the circle by the diameter (d):

If $\pi = \frac{C}{d}$ then $C = \pi d$ or $C = 2\pi r$ (where r is equal to the radius of the circle)

classify

To group things according to type. Classification makes data easier to handle as it reduces the number of things that need to be considered. For example, consider the following shapes:

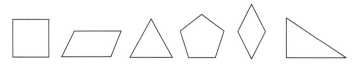

It is possible to consider each shape individually. However, there are occasions when it would be far simpler to consider regular shapes together as a category or irregular shapes as a similar grouping.

clockwise

In the same direction as the hands of a clock travel:

clockwise

column

A vertical arrangement. For example, a column of numbers:

$$24$$
$$45$$
$$168$$
$$73$$
$$841$$

15

common denominator

The denominator of two or more fractions is the same. For example:

$$\frac{2}{9} \quad \frac{5}{9} \quad \frac{7}{9}$$ The common denominator in this example is 9.

common difference

Common difference arises when the difference between any term and the preceding or subsequent term in an arithmetic progression is the same. For example in the arithmetic progression:

the common difference is 5.

common factor

One quantity that is a factor of two or more other numbers. For example:

12 has the factors 1, 2, 3, 4, 6, 12
18 has the factors 1, 2, 3, 6, 9, 18

1, 2, 3, 6 are all common factors of 12 and 18.

commutative law

The order in which the operation is performed makes no difference to the answer. This is true for addition and multiplication:

$$a + b = b + a \qquad a \times b = b \times a$$

It is written generally as:

$$a * b = b * a$$

compare

Comparison in arithmetic usually involves subtraction or division. To compare the numbers 3 and 12 it is possible to say that 12 is 9 more than 3 (subtraction); or 12 is 4 times as much as 3 (division).

compass point

Used to indicate direction:

The position of the four compass points can be remembered using different mnemonics. For example:

Naughty **E**lephants **S**quirt **W**ater

complement

Within any universal set, any set has its own complement. For example, in a class of 30 children 17 walk to school. The complement of this set is the 13 children who do not walk to school.

In number, complements are calculated by subtracting the number from the base. For example, to find the complement of 7 in base 10, simply subtract 7 from 10 to give a complement 3.

complementary angles
(See also **supplementary angles**.)
Two angles that sum to 90°:

composite number
A number which is not a prime number, for example:

6 which has factors 1, 2, 3, 6
18 which has factors 1, 2, 3, 6, 9, 18

compound number
A number expressed in more than one unit – for example, 3 metres 25 centimetres.

concentric
This refers to circles. Circles are concentric if there are two or more of them in the same plane that have the same point for their centre:

concrete number
(See also **abstract number**.)
A number that refers to specific objects – for example, 3 pencils.

cone

A solid with a circular base and a curved surface that finishes with a point (a conical surface). A cone is a rather interesting shape if it is cut. If it is cut horizontally it has a circular cross-section. If it is bisected vertically (i.e. cut in half) it has a triangular cross-section. If it is cut at an angle the cross-section is an ellipse:

congruence/congruent

Shapes are said to be congruent if they are the same shape and size regardless of position and orientation:

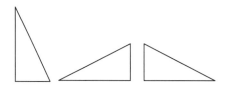

These triangles are congruent: they are the same shape and size. The fact that they are in different positions and orientations does not alter the shape itself.

conjecture

A hypothesis, something that has been surmised or deduced. Once proven it becomes a theorem. Hence 'Fermat's last theorem' should technically have been known as 'Fermat's last conjecture' until Andrew Wiles managed finally to prove it in 1995!

consecutive

Following one after another without interruption. For example, four consecutive numbers would be 3, 4, 5, 6 or the first six consecutive prime numbers are 2, 3, 5, 7, 11, 13.

conservation

The fact that a quantity of matter or a number remain unchanged regardless of its arrangement:

• • • • • • •

• •
•   •
•   •
•

There are still the same number of counters, even though the arrangement has been changed.

continuous data

Data that is measured. Every item of data can be placed along a continuum – for example, the height of bean plants.

co-ordinates

(See **Cartesian co-ordinates**.)

Copernicus, Nicholas (1473–1543)

A Polish astronomer and mathematician. In about 1513 he wrote a short account of what has since become known as the Copernican theory. He proposed that the Sun (not the Earth) is at rest in the centre of the Universe. His heliocentric structure involved giving several distinct motions to the Earth. This was considered implausible by the vast majority of his contemporaries who thought that, if the Earth was moving as suggested by Copernicus, we would all fly off into space! His theory did have its defenders, most notably Johannes Kepler and Galileo Galilei. Strong theoretical support for the Copernican theory was finally provided by Newton's theory of universal gravitation (1687).

corresponding angles

These are angles that have the same relative position in geometric figures. Broadly, they can be considered in two ways. First by looking at parallel lines:

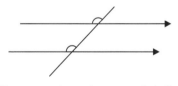

The diagonal line crossing the parallel lines is called a transversal. The intersection of the transversal with the horizontal lines makes lots of angles. Two angles are corresponding angles if they are at corresponding positions in the diagram. Corresponding angles are always equal. In this diagram one pair of corresponding angles has been marked. There are a further three pairs that could also be identified.

The other way to consider corresponding angles is within a geometric shape:

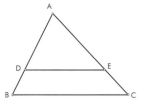

In the diagram above there are two triangles – the large triangle ABC and the small triangle AD̂E. The angles AB̂C and AD̂E are corresponding because they are both in the same relative position in the two triangles. They are also equal in size.

counter-example
Disproving an assertion by finding an exception. For example, the statement 'the sum of three consecutive numbers is always even' can be disproved by showing a counter-example:

$$4 + 5 + 6 = 15$$

counting numbers
(Also called **natural numbers**.)
The set of numbers $\{0, 1, 2, 3, 4, 5, 6...\}$. This set is represented by the symbol C. Some people do not include zero in the set of counting numbers – the arguments continue within the mathematical community!

cube
A regular solid with six square faces – one of the Platonic solids:

cuboid
A solid with six rectangular faces (if the faces are all square it is a cube):

cumulative frequency
A table displaying the running total of a set of data.

cumulative frequency curve
A graph of the running total of a set of data.

cylinder
A solid with one curved surface joining the edges of two circles of equal radius or two identical ellipses:

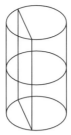

If cut parallel to the base, a circle-based cylinder would have a circular cross-section. If cut perpendicular to the base it would have a rectangular (or square) cross-section.

data
A set of facts, numbers or information frequently displayed in tables or graphs to show the relationship between them.

database
A collection of information organised in such a way that a computer program can quickly select desired pieces of data – a sort of electronic filing system. Traditional databases are organised by fields, records and files. A field is a single piece of information; a record is one complete set of fields; and a file is a collection of records.

decimal/decimal fraction
A fractional number expressed using places to the right of the decimal point.

decimal place
In a decimal number the decimal place is the place a digit occupies relative to the decimal point.

decimal point
A point separating digits with a value greater than one from those with a value less than one.

units · tenths hundredths thousandths

decimal point

deduction
A conclusion based on a set of true statements.

degree
A unit of angular measure (turn) in geometry – symbol °. There are 360° in a full turn. The Greek astronomer Hipparchus of Nicea (c. 170–125 BCE) is believed to have first divided a circle

into 360°. He is thought to have obtained the number 360 from the early astronomers. They believed the Earth was stationary and all the stars rotated about it on a circular band divided into twelve parts. Each part was about 30 days (approximately one lunar cycle) – hence 30 × 12, which gives 360. He did a great deal of work studying the Earth and calculated the length of a year to within 6½ minutes of the figure we accept today!

denary system
A base-10 system.

denominator
The bottom digit in a fraction, representing the number of fractional parts the unit has been divided into:

$$\frac{1}{2} \leftarrow \text{denominator}$$

Descartes, René
Frequently referred to as the 'father of modern mathematics'. He developed the co-ordinate system called Cartesian co-ordinates. This united algebra and geometry as it allowed any equation to be mapped on to a graph as a set of points.

descending order
Decreasing in size. For example, if the numbers 2, 5, 1, 7, 9, 3 were written in descending order they would read 9, 7, 5, 3, 2, 1.

diagonal
In two dimensions a diagonal is a straight line joining two non-adjacent (i.e. not next-door) vertices. In three dimensions it is a straight line joining opposite vertices which do not share a common face (also called a space diagonal).

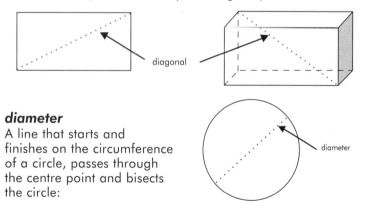

diagonal

diameter
A line that starts and finishes on the circumference of a circle, passes through the centre point and bisects the circle:

diameter

difference
The amount by which one quantity is greater or less than another quantity. Difference is calculated using subtraction.

digit
In Hindu–Arabic notation, the digits are 0, 1, 2, 3, 4, 5, 6, 7, 8, 9. Many numbers have more than one digit. For example, the number 275 has three digits 2, 7 and 5.

dihedral angle
This is the angle between two intersecting planes. In a polyhedron it is the angle at an edge formed between the two faces:

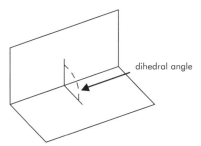

Diophantus c. (200–c. 284)
Often referred to as the 'father of algebra'. He wrote *Arithmetica* which contained thirteen volumes on the solution of algebraic equations. He introduced a new notation system using contractions or symbols to stand for unknown quantities.

discrete data
This is data that can be counted. Every item of data can be placed in a category – for example, colours of cars.

distribution
When the values of data are arranged in order this is called a distribution. For example the following array is the distribution for a set of children's tests scores:

56 57 57 60 61 61 64 64
65 66 67 68 69 69 70 70

distributive law
One operation is 'distributed out' over another operation. This is true for multiplication over addition and multiplication over subtraction:

$$a \times (b + c) = (a \times b) + (a \times c) \qquad a \times (b - c) = (a \times b) - (a \times c)$$

It is also true that division is 'right distributive' over addition and subtraction (i.e. the division needs to be on the right side of the brackets):

$$(a + b) \div c = (a \div c) + (b \div c) \quad (a - b) \div c = (a \div c) - (b \div c)$$

divide
(See **division**.)

dividend
Within the operation of division, the number that is divided by another number. For example in the division $24 \div 6$, 24 is the dividend. (See also **division** and **divisor**.)

divine proportion
(See **golden section**.)

divisible (by)
If a number (a) can be exactly divided by another number (b), leaving no remainder, then a is said to be divisible by b. For example the number 10 is divisible by both 5 and 2.

division
Is the inverse operation of multiplication. It can be structured as sharing or as grouping. Sharing involves the 'one for me, one for you' idea that it must be equal sharing. Grouping looks at how many groups of a particular size there are in a total number.

divisor
Within the operation of division, the number that divides another number. For example, in the division $24 \div 6$, 6 is the divisor. (See also **dividend** and **division**.)

dodecahedron
A polyhedron with twelve faces. If it is regular it has twelve regular pentagons for the faces and is one of the Platonic solids:

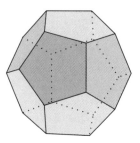

edge

The line where two faces join (i.e. the intersection of two plane faces of a solid):

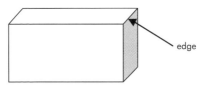

Egyptians

From 3000 BCE the Egyptians developed quite a sophisticated understanding of mathematics. They used fractions, basic algebra, standard units of measurement and geometric concepts within their daily lives.

The Egyptians had a decimal system using seven different symbols.

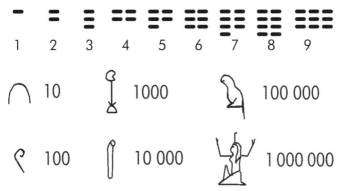

1 is a single stroke
10 is a drawing of a hobble for cattle
100 is a coil of rope
1000 is a lotus plant
10 000 is a finger
100 000 is a tadpole or frog
1 000 000 is the figure of a god with arms raised above his head — also used to indicate 'many'

element

A member of a set. For example, the set {3, 6, 9, 12} has four elements.

enlargement

Each measurement is multiplied by a scale factor in order to enlarge or reduce an image.

equal/equality
The mathematical idea expressed by the $=$ sign. For example, if 3 is added to 4 then the answer is 7. This can be written as $3 + 4 = 7$, the $=$ sign expressing the equality of the two statements.

There are three properties of equality. They are:

- the reflexive property, $a = a$. For example, $4 = 4$ and $627 = 627$;
- the symmetric property, 'if $x = y$ then $y = x$'. For example, $12 = 6 + 6$ and $6 + 6 = 12$;
- the transitive property, 'if $x = y$ and $y = z$ then $x = z$'. For example, if $6 + 6 = 12$ and $12 = 24 \div 2$ then $6 + 6 = 24 \div 2$.

equal chance
The likelihood of different events occurring being the same is known as an equal chance. For example, when flipping a coin it is equally likely that a head or a tail will be achieved.

equally likely
(See **equal chance**.)

equals
(See **equal/equality**.)

equation
A statement that two expressions are equal. For example, $y = x + 2$ is an equation stating that the expression y is equal to the expression $x + 2$.

equilateral triangle
A regular triangle. All sides are of equal length and all interior angles are the same size i.e. $60°$:

equivalent
Having the same value.

equivalent fractions
Fractions that have the same value but that are expressed differently. Because they have the same value they appear on the number line in the same position. For example:

$$^1/_2 = {}^2/_4 = {}^3/_6 \qquad\qquad ^1/_3 = {}^2/_6 = {}^4/_{12}$$

Eratosthenes (c. 276–194 BCE)

A Greek mathematician and librarian at the University of Alexandria. He used a rather ingenious method for calculating the circumference of the Earth and was also very interested in prime numbers. He worked out a method of finding prime numbers which became known as the Sieve of Eratosthenes. If all the prime numbers up to 150 need to be established, Eratosthenes worked out that it was only necessary to consider multiples of every number up to 13. He knew this because any number up to 150 which is not prime would have a factor of 13 or less (because 13 x 13 = 169).

So how does his 'sieve' work? As all primes up to 150 need to be found it is necessary to start with a 150 grid. Starting at 2 (1 is not prime – see **prime number**), put a ring around it as it must be prime. Next shade all the multiples of 2. Then put a ring around the next unshaded number, in this case 3. Now shade in all the multiples of 3. The next unshaded number is 5, which is also prime. Put a ring around it and shade in all the multiples of 5. Do the same with the next unshaded number and so on. Remember to stop once all the multiples of 13 have been shaded. All the numbers left unshaded in the grid at this point must be prime:

1	②	③	4	⑤	6	⑦	8	9	10
⑪	12	⑬	14	15	16	17	18	19	20
21	22	23	24	25	26	27	28	29	30
31	32	33	34	35	36	37	38	39	40
41	42	43	44	45	46	47	48	49	50
51	52	53	54	55	56	57	58	59	60
61	62	63	64	65	66	67	68	69	70
71	72	73	74	75	76	77	78	79	80
81	82	83	84	85	86	87	88	89	90
91	92	93	94	95	96	97	98	99	100
101	102	103	104	105	106	107	108	109	110
111	112	113	114	115	116	117	118	119	120
121	122	123	124	125	126	127	128	129	130
131	132	133	134	135	136	137	138	139	140
141	142	143	144	145	146	147	148	149	150

estimation
The rough answer (a judgement of an approximate value or amount).

Euclid (c. 330–275 BCE)
A Greek mathematician famous for his books *Elements*. These were a collection of theorems, problems and proofs. His work was so influential that the geometry of points, lines, shapes and solids is referred to as Euclidean geometry. He also proved that there is an infinite number of prime numbers. Some very large primes have been calculated using computers. At the time of writing the largest known prime number is $2^{13466917} - 1$ which has 4053946 digits!

Euler's formula
Named after the Swiss mathematician, Leonhard Euler (1707–83). Euler's formula states that the sum of the number of vertices and faces of a solid is 2 more than the number of edges. For example, a cube:

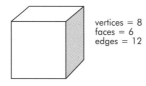

vertices = 8
faces = 6
edges = 12

vertices + faces = edges + 2
8 + 6 = 12 + 2

Euler's formula is true for a great number of solid shapes and should certainly hold for all solids encountered in a primary classroom.

even
An even number has 2 as one of its factors.

even chance
(See **equal chance**.)

exactly
Leaving no remainder.

exchange
Exchange is a fundamental part of our place value structure. As the columns go from right to left an exchange can take place which ensures that any number, no matter how large, can be written using only the digits 0, 1, 2, 3, 4, 5, 6, 7, 8, 9. So 10 ones (or units) can be exchanged for 1 ten, 10 tens for 1 hundred and so on.

exhaustion
A proof that is arrived at by considering all possibilities.

experimental probability
The number between 0 and 1 that is found by dividing the number of outcomes by the total number of trials.

exponent
The power to which a number has been raised. For example, $10 \times 10 \times 10$ can be recorded as 10^3 where the 3 is the exponent.

expression
A general term used to describe mathematical terms – for example, x^2 or $3x + 2$.

exterior angle
An angle created outside a polygon by lengthening one of the sides. For example:

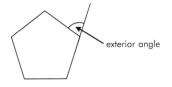

exterior angle

face
The flat surface of a solid shape (i.e. parts of planes):

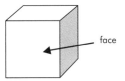

face

factor
A number that divides another number exactly (e.g. 8 is a factor of 32, but 5 is not).

Fermat, Pierre de (1601–1665)
A French lawyer who was passionate about mathematics. Fermat's last theorem concerned Pythagorean triples – three whole numbers that satisfy the equation:

$$a^2 + b^2 = c^2 \text{ e.g. } 3^2 + 4^2 = 5^2 \text{ or } 5^2 + 12^2 = 13^2$$

His theorem was actually a conjecture hypothesising that there could be no triples if a, b and c were raised to any power higher than 2, such as $a^3 + b^3 = c^3$. The problem tantalised mathematicians for 350 years until finally, in 1995, Andrew Wiles of Cambridge solved it.

Fibonacci numbers – Fibonacci (or Leonardo of Pisa, 1170–1250)

Fibonacci, short for filius Bonacci, meaning 'son of Bonacci' (like John-son in English), was an Italian mathematician. He was one of the first people to introduce the Hindu–Arabic decimal number system into Europe. He is best known for a sequence of numbers called the Fibonacci sequence. This sequence of numbers was generated when he posed the following problem in his book, *Liber Abaci*:

> *a pair of rabbits are put in a field and, if rabbits take a month to become mature and then produce a new pair every month after that, how many pairs will there be in twelve months time?*

Assuming the rabbits do not escape and none die the answer is the following sequence of numbers:

$$1, 1, 2, 3, 5, 8, 13, 21, \ldots$$

As can be seen from the sequence, each term is generated by adding the two preceding terms together. The Fibonacci sequence can be observed in many different situations in the natural world – for example the number of segments in the spirals on a pineapple or the number of 'petals' in the spirals on a pine cone or seeds in the spirals in a sunflower head:

formula
A rule, usually expressed as an equation.

fraction
A fraction is expressed as the quotient of two numbers: the dividend is the numerator, the divisor the denominator.

frequency histogram
A graph displaying continuous data grouped into classes.

frequency table
A table identifying the frequency of data:

Shoe size	Number of children
1	2
2	4
3	6
4	7
5	8
6	3
7	1

function
A rule that changes or maps one number on to another.

Galilei, Galileo (1564–1642)
An Italian mathematician and astronomer. He built a telescope with which he discovered the four moons of Jupiter. He was a great supporter of the Copernican theory of the solar system. Indeed, his support for the idea that the Earth was not at the centre of the universe resulted in him being sent into exile in 1633.

Gelosia multiplication
This method of multiplication dates back to twelfth-century India. It is also sometimes called 'Chinese' multiplication, 'lattice' multiplication or 'grating' multiplication. This method depends on producing a grid so that place value is implicit within the structure. Take the example of 35×24:

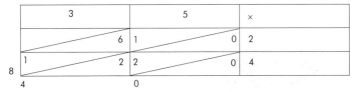

The digits at the top of the grid are multiplied in turn by those down the side. The answers to each of these multiplications are written in the boxes, the tens value being written above the diagonal and the units value below. Finally, the numbers in each diagonal are added, carrying as necessary to the next diagonal.

geometry
The area of mathematics that deals with the relationships, properties and measurements of solids, surfaces, lines and angles. It also includes the study of space with regard to spatial relationships and figures in space.

golden section

(See also **Fibonacci numbers**.)

A line divided into two parts such that the ratio of the short part to the long part is equal to the ratio of the long part to the whole line. Numerically the ratio is approximately 1:0.61803. This gives the ratio a value of about 1.161803. This value for the golden section is called Ø (phi). The ratio gives rise to shapes that are felt to be most pleasing to the eye. The Egyptians used the golden section ratio in the design of the pyramids, the Greeks in the Parthenon and many other buildings, the Renaissance artists used it to ensure beauty and balance in their art, it was used in the design of Notre Dame in Paris and in the United Nations Building in New York. Equally, when the time spans of different sections of a piece of music are proportional to the golden ratio, the piece seems more pleasing to listen to.

The golden section is also found in many naturally occurring situations – the rows of petals in flowers or the spirals in seashells:

The human body is also a source of the golden section. The ratio of the forearm to hand is phi. The hand creates a golden section in relation to the arm, as the ratio of the forearm to the hand is 1.618. Amazingly, the double helix spiral of the DNA molecule is also based on the golden section:

The Fibonacci series can be used to calculate phi:

1, 1, 2, 3, 5, 8, 13, 21, 34, 55, 89, 144, ...

The ratio of each successive pair of numbers in the series is a closer and closer approximation to phi – for example, 5 divided by 3 is 1.666..., and 8 divided by 5 is 1.60. The 40th number in the series (102334155) divided by the 39th (63245986), gives a ratio that is accurate to 15 decimal places – 1.618033988749895...

To find a handy golden section, look no further than the average wallet! Standard-sized credit cards are 54 mm by 86 mm, creating a ratio of 1:0.628, less than a millimetre away from a perfect golden section of 1:0.618.

googol/googolplex
- googol: 10^{100}, or 1 followed by 100 zeros
- googolplex: $10^{10^{100}}$, or 10^{googol}, or 1 followed by a googol zeros

The names for these very large but finite numbers were created by the 9-year-old nephew of Edward Kasner (1878- 1955), an American mathematician.

gradient
The slope of a graph. To calculate the gradient (often called m) of a straight line, it is necessary to know the co-ordinates of two points. Taking $y = 3x$, the points $(-2, -6)$ and $(1, 3)$ lie on the graph. To calculate the gradient the differences must be found between the y co-ordinates (a) and the x coordinates (b), then the difference in the y coordinates is divided by the difference in the x coordinates, i.e. $a \div b$:

$$\text{gradient } (m) = \frac{a}{b} = \frac{(3--6)}{(1--2)} = \frac{9}{3} = 3$$

This value is equal to the value that x was multiplied by in the original equation, i.e. $y = 3x$:

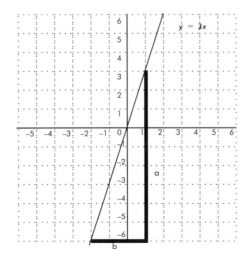

graph
A diagrammatic illustration of data. It is frequently a series of points plotted along two axes.

greater than

An inequality between numbers. The symbol used to represent 'greater than' is > with the 'arrow' pointing towards the smallest number. For example, 12 > 9 means 12 is greater than 9. (See also **less than**.)

greater than or equal to

Inequalities are frequently encountered within algebra – for example, $x > 6$ which means x can take any value greater than 6. However, if it is written as $x \geqslant 6$ it reads as x is 'greater than or equal to' 6, which means that x can take any value greater than 6 or equal to 6 itself. (See also **less than or equal to**.)

Greeks

The Greeks separated mathematics into *mathematica*, which was pure mathematics, and *arithmetica*, which was practical mathematics. This clearly demonstrated an enjoyment and appreciation of 'maths for maths sake'. The Greeks founded a great library at Alexandria (then under Greek rule) with the backing of Ptolemy Soter. The library became renowned as a place of study for mathematics. Indeed, Archimedes, Euclid, Diophantus and Hypatia all worked and studied there. The library contained over 500,000 manuscripts in the form of scrolls and books. When visiting Alexandria all ships were searched for books. If any were found they were taken to the library for copying. The library then kept the original and returned the copy!

The Greek number system changed from the classical age to the Alexandrian age. In the classical age, the system involved tallying and letters:

$$| = 1 \quad || = 2 \quad ||| = 3 \quad |||| = 4.$$

$\Gamma = 5$ the symbol Γ is a form of the Greek letter π, the first letter of the Greek word for five: *penta*

$\Gamma| = 6$ and so on

$\Delta = 10$ the symbol Δ is a form of the Greek letter δ, the first letter of the Greek word for ten: *deka*

$\Delta\Delta = 20$

$\Gamma^\Delta = 50$ from 5×10

$\Gamma^\Delta\Delta = 60$

$H = 100$ the symbol H is a form of the Greek letter η, the first letter of the Greek word for hundred: *hekaton*

$\Gamma^{H} = 500$ from 5×100

X = 1000	the symbol X is a form of the Greek letter χ, the first letter of the Greek word for thousand: *khilioi*
M = 10 000	the symbol M is a form of the Greek letter μ, the first letter of the Greek word for ten thousand: *murioi*

In the Alexandrian age the number system changed to using the alphabet to represent numbers. This was very cumbersome and meant that over 27 different symbols had to be used.

grid multiplication
Another way of tackling multiplication which illustrates how multiplication is underpinned by the distributive law. It involves a tabular form of calculation. For example, 24×35:

×	30	5	
20	600	100	700
4	120	20	140
			840

helix
(Plural, helices.)
A 3-D spiral which lies around either a cylinder or a cone.

hemi-sphere
Half a sphere:

heptagon
A seven-sided polygon. For example:

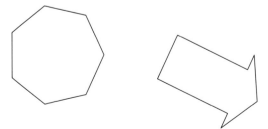

hexagon
A six-sided polygon. For example:

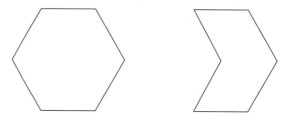

highest common factor
A common factor is a quantity that is a factor of two or more other numbers. for example:

12 has the factors 1, 2, 3, 4, 6, 12
18 has the factors 1, 2, 3, 6, 9, 18

1, 2, 3, 6 are all common factors of 12 and 18, with 6 being the highest common factor.

Hindu–Arabic numerals
So called as they are based upon an ancient Hindu system. This system was further developed by Arab traders as they travelled throughout the ninth and tenth centuries. It then spread into Europe where this base-10 number system was adopted. The ten digits of the Hindu–Arabic system are 0, 1, 2, 3, 4, 5, 6, 7, 8, 9, with 0 acting as a place holder.

horizontal
A horizontal line or surface lies at $0°$ or $180°$ – i.e. it lies flat.

Hypatia of Alexandria (c. 370–415)
The daughter of Theon, a mathematician at Alexandria. She too taught mathematics and also wrote widely. Her most important work was a commentary on Diophantus' *Arithmetica*. In 415 she refused to convert to Christianity and, after being violently set upon, she was brutally murdered.

hypotenuse
The longest side of a right-angled triangle. It is the side that is opposite the right angle:

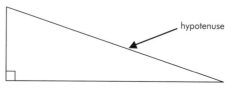

hypotenuse

icosahedron

A polyhedron with twenty faces. If it is regular it has twenty equilateral triangles for the faces and is one of the Platonic solids:

imperial system

A system of measures introduced in the Magna Carta in 1215:

Measure	Unit
Mass	16 ounces (oz) = 1 pound (lb)
	14 pounds = 1 stone
	112 pounds = 1 hundredweight (cwt)
Length	12 inches (in) = 1 foot (ft)
	3 feet = 1 yard (yd)
	1760 yards = 1 mile
Area	144 square inches (sq. in.) = 1 square foot (sq ft)
	9 square feet = 1 square yard (sq yd)
	4840 square yards = 1 acre (A)
	640 acres = 1 square mile (sq mi)
Volume	1728 cubic inches (cu in) = 1 cubic foot (cu ft)
	27 cubic feet = 1 cubic yard (cu yd)
Capacity	4 gills (gi) = 1 pint (pt)
	2 pints = 1 quart (qt)
	4 quarts (8 pints) = 1 gallon

improper fraction

A fraction which has a numerator that is larger than the denominator – for example $^5/_3$, $^8/_5$. Fractions in which the numerator and denominator are equal are also usually considered improper – for example $^2/_2$, $^5/_5$.

independent events

Events when the outcome of one event does not affect the outcome of another event – for example, tossing two coins.

index form

A concise way of writing repeated multiplication of a number by itself. For example, $10 \times 10 \times 10 \times 10 = 10^4$, the index is 4 (see also **base** and **power**).

inequality

A statement that one quantity is greater or less than another.

integer

Positive integers are all the whole numbers greater than zero: 1, 2, 3, 4, 5, ... Negative integers are all the opposites of these whole numbers: -1, -2, -3, -4, -5, ... We do not consider zero to be a positive or negative number. However, it is an integer. For each positive integer, there is a negative integer, and these integers are called opposites. For example, -3 is the opposite of 3, -21 is the opposite of 21, and 8 is the opposite of -8. The set of integers is represented by the symbol I, positive integers by I_p and negative integers by I_n.

interior angle

The angles on the inside (interior) of a polygon:

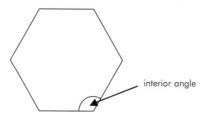

interior angle

interquartile range

The interval between the upper quartile and the lower quartile in a set of data.

inverse

Subtraction is the inverse of addition and division is the inverse of multiplication and vice versa. Square numbers and square roots, cube numbers and cube roots, and so forth, are also inverse.

investigate

The process of investigation involves critical thinking, mathematical confidence, the application of learned knowledge and the acquisition of new knowledge. The process allows for uncertainty, conflict and doubt, which provide the motivation that leads to a continuous search for resolution and contributes to a more refined understanding of the mathematical world.

irrational number

The set of numbers that cannot be expressed in fractional form – for example $\sqrt{2}$, π, e. The set of irrational numbers (together with the set of rational numbers) gives the set of real numbers. The symbol used to represent the set of irrational numbers is: $\bar{R}$.

irregular

An irregular polygon is one in which not all the sides are the same length and not all the angles are the same size:

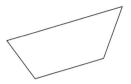

isosceles triangle

A triangle which has two sides of equal length. As well as having two sides of equal length, an isosceles triangle also has two angles of equal size. An isosceles triangle has one line of reflective symmetry and rotational symmetry of order one. The name isosceles derives from the Greek *iso* (same) and *skelos* (leg).

Jones, William (1675–1749)

Born in Llanfihangel Tw'r Beird, Anglesey, Wales, in 1675 William Jones taught mathematics and wrote about a range of topics including calculus and navigation. He is most noted for being the first person to use π to represent the ratio of the circumference to the diameter of a circle.

Kepler, Johannes (1571–1630)

A German astronomer who discovered that all the planets of the solar system had elliptical orbits and not circular paths as previously believed. He also described three laws of planetary motion and is considered one of the founders of modern astronomy.

kite

A quadrilateral that has two adjacent pairs of sides that are equal in length, and at least one pair of opposite angles are equal. The diagonals cross at right angles. A kite has at least one line of reflective symmetry. A rhombus and a square can also be considered a kite:

L

Lagrange, Joseph Louis (1736–1813)

Generally considered a French mathematician although Lagrange was born in Italy. A prolific writer, he was also head of the Committee on Weights and Measures which adopted the metric system.

less than

An inequality between numbers. The symbol used to represent 'less than' is < with the 'arrow' pointing towards the smallest number. For example, 9 < 12 means 9 is less than 12. (See also **greater than**.)

less than or equal to

Inequalities are frequently encountered within algebra, for example $x < 6$ which means x can take any value less than 6. However, if it is written as $x \leq 6$ it reads as x is 'less than or equal to' 6, which means that x can take any value less than 6 or equal to 6 itself. (See also **greater than or equal to**.)

like terms

Multiples of the same algebraic quantity. Hence if terms are not of the same algebraic quantity they are unlike terms. For example:

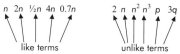

line

A particular set of points. In geometry lines are straight (unless otherwise stated) and extend in two directions without end. Finite lines are more correctly referred to as line segments.

line graph

A graph used to display continuous data, where curves or line segments join points of measured data.

line of symmetry

(See **axis of symmetry**.)

linear equation

Takes the form $ay + bx + c = 0$. A linear equation can always be represented as a straight line graph.

lower quartile

The value one quarter of the way along a set of ordered data.

lowest common multiple (LCM)

When considering two or more integers, the lowest common

multiple is the smallest number that can be divided exactly by each of the integers. For example, the lowest common multiple of 4 and 6 is 12.

magic square

Magic squares are descendants of the oldest known number mystery, the legend of Lo Shu, found in China in a book entitled *Yih King*. This first magic square is over 3000 years old. In a magic square all the rows, columns and diagonals add to the same total. For example:

8	1	6
3	5	7
4	9	2

mapping

A function is a rule that maps one number on to another. The first set of numbers is called the domain. Elements in this set are mapped on to those in the second set, the range. Mappings can have a one-to-one relationship, i.e. each member of the domain corresponds to one member of the range; or a many-to-one relation, in which more than one member of the domain corresponds to a particular member of the range. Whether one-to-one or many-to-one, each member of the domain only ever corresponds to one member of the range. A 'function machine' (as encountered in many primary schools) is a simple way of representing mappings.

mass

The amount of matter contained in an object.

Mayan number system

The Mayan civilisation spanned the period from about 2000 BCE to 900. They used a base-20 (vigesimal) number system. This system involved three symbols, together with a place value concept to represent numbers. The symbols were:

0	1	5

Having a symbol for zero together with a place value structure meant that Mayans could represent any number in quite a straightforward manner.

0	1	2	3	4
5	6	7	8	9
10	11	12	13	14
15	16	17	18	19

Larger numbers were written as powers of 20 and recorded vertically:

this represents the number 20. The dot shows there is one in the 20s 'row', the shell that there is zero in the units 'row'.

31 would be written as:

20
11

after the 20s 'row' was full with 19×20 the next row was actually 360s and not 400s as might be expected in a true base-20 system. The number 360 is derived from 20×18 (it is also the number of days in one of their years). The rows then carry on systematically, the next being 18×20^2, 18×20^3 and so forth.

Hence 9542 would be written as:

$$\left.\begin{array}{l} 7200 \\ 2160 \ (6 \times 360) \\ 180 \ (9 \times 20) \\ 2 \end{array}\right\} 9542$$

mean
The sum of the values in a set of data divided by the total number of items in that set.

median
The middle value of a set of ordered data. For example, in the set 2, 3, 5, 6, 9 the median is 5. If a set of data has an even number of items with no single middle number, then the median is the mean of the two middle numbers.

metric system

A measurement system designed by French scientists in the late eighteenth century. It was designed to ensure consistency and to replace the wide range of measures in use at the time. In order to obtain a standard unit of length, a quadrant of the earth (one fourth of a circumference) was measured from Dunkirk to Barcelona along the meridian that passes through Paris. The distance from the pole to the equator was divided into ten million parts in order to establish a length for the metre. The definition of the metre has become more and more precise throughout the years. A metre is currently taken to be the distance light travels in a vacuum in $1/299\,792\,458$ second. Units used in the metric system include:

Mass	gram (g), kilogram (kg), tonne
Length	millimetre (mm), centimetre (cm), metre (m), kilometre (km)
Area	square centimetre (cm^2), square metre (m^2), square kilometre (km^2)
Volume	cubic centimetre (cm^3), cubic metre (m^3)
Capacity	millilitre (ml), litre (l)

minuend

The quantity from which another quantity is to be subtracted.

minus

The name for the symbol $-$. Hence 9 minus 3 is written as $9 - 3$ and means that 3 is subtracted from 9.

mirror line

(See **axis of symmetry**.)

mixed number

If the improper fractions $5/3$ and $8/5$ are simplified they give $1\,2/3$ and $1\,3/5$ respectively. These numbers (with a mix of whole numbers and fractional parts) are called mixed numbers.

Möbius strip

The Möbius Strip gets its name from the German mathematician, August Ferdinand Möbius (1790–1860). The interesting thing about the Möbius Strip is that unlike most other 2-D surfaces (such as a page of this book) it has only one 'side'. It is made by giving a half-twist to a strip of paper and then fastening the ends. If a line is drawn down the middle of the strip it will come back to the starting point having covered both 'sides' of the paper, without lifting the pencil – hence it must actually have only one 'side':

mode

The value that occurs most often in a set of data. For example in the following set of data the mode is 5:

shoe sizes 1, 2, 2, 3, 4, 5, 5, 5, 6, 7

multiple

The product of a given number with another factor. For example, multiples of 4 are 4 (1×4), 8 (2×4), 12 (3×4)...

multiplicand

The name given to one number that is being multiplied by another number (called the multiplier). For example:

$$45 \times 21$$

multiplicand   multiplier

multiplier

(See **multiplicand**.)

multiply

Can be considered as a shorthand notation for a longer calculation. For example, if there are 6 bags each containing 5 sweets it would be possible to solve this by tackling it as repeated addition (i.e. $5 + 5 + 5 + 5 + 5 + 5$). However, this is quite a long and rather tedious calculation. Hence the shorter 6×5 is far more useful, particularly as calculations get bigger – imagine trying to write 2637×4328 as a repeated addition!

mutually exclusive events

Events which, having happened, exclude any other outcome from occurring in that same event. For example throwing a 3 on a die excludes a 1, 2, 4, 5 or 6 being thrown at the same time.

Napier, John (1550–1617)

A Scottish aristocrat who developed logarithms. He is also known for his invention of Napier's Bones, which are used for multiplication calculations:

	0	1	2	3	4	5	6	7	8	9
1	0	1	2	3	4	5	6	7	8	9
2	0	2	4	6	8 1	0 1	2 1	4 1	6 1	8
3	0	3	6	9 1	2 1	5 1	8 2	1 2	4 2	7
4	0	4	8 1	2 1	6 2	0 2	4 2	8 3	2 3	6
5	0	5 1	0 1	5 2	0 2	5 3	0 3	5 4	0 4	5
6	0	6 1	2 1	8 2	4 3	0 3	6 4	2 4	8 5	4
7	0	7 1	4 2	1 2	8 3	5 4	2 4	9 5	6 6	3
8	0	8 1	6 2	4 3	2 4	0 4	8 5	6 6	4 7	2
9	0	9 1	8 2	7 3	6 4	5 5	4 6	3 7	2 8	1

Having created the 'bones' as above it is then quite straightforward to rearrange certain columns in order to undertake multiplication calculations. For example, to work out 253×6:

	2	5	3
1	2	5	3
2	4 1	0	6
3	6 1	5	9
4	8 2	0 1	2
5 1	0 2	5 1	5
6 1	2 3	0 1	8
7 1	4 3	5 2	1
8 1	6 4	0 2	4
9 1	8 4	5 2	7

To complete the calculation it necessary to focus on the one row identified above and reproduced here:

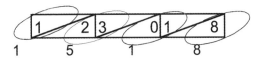

Hence the answer to the question 253×6 is 1518. A logical progression from here is to consider the **Gelosia** method for long multiplication.

natural numbers
(Also called counting numbers and whole numbers.)
The set of numbers {0, 1, 2, 3, 4, 5, 6...}. This set is represented by the symbol N. Some people do not include zero

in the set of natural numbers – the arguments continue within the mathematical community!

negative
Numbers which are less than zero. For any positive number there exists an additive inverse. This is a negative number which, when added to the original positive number, gives an answer of zero. For example -8 is the additive inverse of 8 because $8 + (-8) = 0$.

net
A flat shape that can be folded to form a solid. For example, one possible net for a cube is:

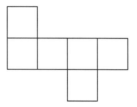

Newton, Sir Isaac (1642–1727)
An English mathematician and physicist. He discovered the universal law of gravitation and also established three laws of motion. He is also credited with work on calculus, although whether he or Leibniz actually invented it is still hotly debated within the mathematics community!

number
A concept of quantity. Symbolic representations (numerals) are used to indicate the number or amount of something.

number bonds
Tend to apply to addition. For example, the number bonds for 10 are:

$$10 + 0 = 10$$
$$9 + 1 = 10$$
$$8 + 2 = 10$$
$$7 + 3 = 10$$
$$6 + 4 = 10$$
$$5 + 5 = 10$$
$$4 + 6 = 10$$
$$3 + 7 = 10$$
$$2 + 8 = 10$$
$$1 + 9 = 10$$
$$0 + 10 = 10$$

number facts
Addition, subtraction, multiplication and division facts related to number.

number sentence
Expresses a complete mathematical thought. For example:

$$2 + 3 = 5 \qquad 9 < 12 \qquad 6 \times 4 = 24 \qquad y = 7$$

numeral
The symbolic representation of a number.

numerator
The top digit in a fraction representing the number of fractional parts. For example:

$$\frac{1}{2} \leftarrow \text{numerator}$$

oblong
A rectangle which is not a square. For example:

obtuse angle
An angle that is greater than 90° but less than 180°. For example:

obtuse angle

octagon
An eight-sided polygon. For example:

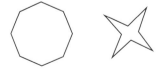

octahedron
A polyhedron with eight faces. If it is regular it has eight equilateral triangles for the faces and is one of the Platonic solids. For example:

47

odd
A whole number that does not have 2 as a factor.

operation
The rules for combining numbers. For example, addition, subtraction, multiplication and division are all operations encountered within primary schools.

order of precedence
(See **BODMAS**.)

ordered pair
Two numbers in which the order is important – for example (6, 4) and (4, 6) are examples of ordered pairs.

ordering
Putting a collection of items in order from smallest to biggest/ biggest to smallest according to mass, length, thickness, etc.

ordinal number
Specifies the order or position of a member of a set. For example:

first   second   third

ordinate
The second number in a pair of Cartesian co-ordinates. The ordinate always represents the distance along the y-axis.

origin
The point where the x and y-axes intersect. It has the Cartesian co-ordinates (0, 0).

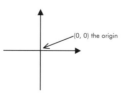

(0, 0) the origin

Oughtred, William (1575–1660)
An English mathematician who introduced the symbols × for multiplication and : for proportion.

parallel
Lines travelling in the same direction but which will never meet.

parallelogram
A quadrilateral which has pairs of opposite sides equal in length and parallel, and the opposite angles are equal in size. The diagonals bisect each other. Parallelograms have rotational symmetry of at least order 2. Why 'at least'? There are some other quadrilaterals which fit the general description of a parallelogram but which have different symmetry properties:

Pascal, Blaise (1623–1662)
A French mathematician who developed Pascal's Triangle. The triangle had been known about for around 600 years. However, it was Pascal who discovered the links between various sequences and series and the properties of the table.

```
                        1
                     1     1
                  1     2     1
               1     3     3     1
            1     4     6     4     1
         1     5    10    10     5     1
      1     6    15    20    15     6     1
   1     7    21    35    35    21     7     1
1     8    28    56    70    56    28     8     1
```

pattern
Mathematics is about the study and representation of patterns. Mathematicians seek and use patterns in order to aid their calculations and to generalise observations and prove hypotheses.

pentagon
A five-sided polygon. For example:

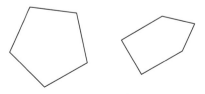

percentage

Fractions with a denominator of 100. They can also be represented as decimals – for example, $\frac{1}{4} = \frac{25}{100} = 0.25 = 25\%$.

perfect number

An integer equal to the sum of all its factors except the integer itself. For example, 6 is perfect because $1 + 2 + 3 = 6$, as is 28 because $1 + 2 + 4 + 7 + 14 = 28$.

perimeter

The total length of the sides bounding an area. For example:

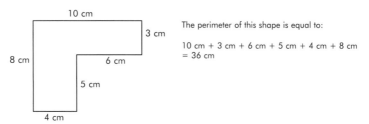

The perimeter of this shape is equal to:

10 cm + 3 cm + 6 cm + 5 cm + 4 cm + 8 cm
= 36 cm

perpendicular

Two lines are said to be perpendicular if they meet at right angles.

pi (π)

(See also **circle**.)

An irrational number found when the circumference of a circle is divided by the diameter. It is approximately equal to 3.141592... The value of π has been calculated with ever-increasing accuracy. The ancient Egyptian 'Rhind Papyrus' has the earliest recording of a value for π of $\frac{256}{81}$, which is about 3.16049. Archimedes calculated π as 3.1419, which is close to today's value. In 1989 the Chudnovsky brothers found π to a billion digits! In 1997 Kanada and Takahasi calculated it to 51½ billion digits!

pictogram

A graph used to display discrete data where one picture/symbol can represent one or many item(s) of data:

The most popular way of coming to school

Bus	☺ ☺ ☺
Car	☺ ☺ ☺ ☺ ☺ ☺ ☺ ☺
Walk	☺ ☺ ☺ ☺ ☺ ☺ ☺ ☺ ☺ ☺ ☺ ☺
Bike	☺ ☺

pie chart
A circle graph cut into sectors:

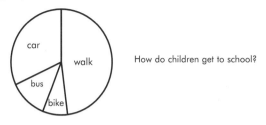

How do children get to school?

place value
(See also **zero**.)
Place value is used by number systems that allow the same digit to carry different values based on its position – i.e. the *place* has a particular *value*. The position of a digit relative to any other digits determines its value. In our base-10 place-value system the larger groupings are always on the left. To identify the size of a number you need to work out the value of each of the digits and then add them – for example, in 358, the 3 represents 300, the 5 represents 50 and the 8 is 8 ones. The total value of the whole number is the sum of these values, 300 + 50 + 8 = 358.

plane
A flat surface extending infinitely in all directions.

Plato (429–347 BCE)
A teacher in ancient Greece and a pupil of Socrates. Plato, rather like Pythagoras, felt that the secret of the universe was to be found in number and geometry. Above the entrance to his school he had written the following words: 'Let none ignorant of geometry enter my door.'

platonic solid
The five regular polyhedra, comprising the regular tetrahedron, the cube, the regular octahedron, the regular dodecahedron and the regular icosahedron. The Platonic solids have been known since the time of the ancient Greeks. They were described by Plato in 350 BCE and, hence, now bear his name. The fact that there can only be five was proved by Euclid. Euler's formula can be applied to all the Platonic solids.

plot
To position a point using its co-ordinates.

plus
The name for the symbol +. Hence, 9 plus 3 is written as 9 + 3 and means that 3 is added to 9.

polygon

A plane shape with straight sides and many angles. Polygon comes from the Greek *poly* meaning 'many', and *gon* from *gonu* meaning 'knees'. So a polygon is a shape with many knees! It would be possible to keep naming polygons indefinitely and scholars have worked out systems to keep naming polygons up to those with millions of sides. However, within primary mathematics it is more usual to deal with polygons up to a dodecagon (12 sides):

Number of sides	Name
3	triangle (sometimes referred to as a trigon for mathematical consistency)
4	quadrilateral (sometimes referred to as a tetragon for mathematical consistency)
5	pentagon
6	hexagon
7	heptagon
8	octagon
9	enneagon (frequently referred to as a nonagon)
10	decagon
11	hendecagon
12	dodecagon

polyhedron

(Plural polyhedra.)
A solid formed from many flat faces. Polyhedron comes from *poly* meaning 'many' and *hedron* from the Indo-European word meaning 'seat'. Hence a polyhedron is a shape with many seats. Naming polyhedra is as systematic as naming polygons. In primary schools you will encounter polyhedra with a greater number of faces than 12. The following will help in systematically working out the names of polyhedra (incidentally, the 'kai' here means 'and'):

1	mono
2	di
3	tri
4	tetra
5	penta
6	hexa
7	hepta
8	octa
9	ennea
10	deca
11	hendeca
12	dodeca
13	triskaideca

14 tetrakaideca
19 enneakaideca
20 icosa
21 icosikaihena
22 icosikaidi
23 icosikaitri

29 icosikaiennea
30 triaconta
31 triacontakaihena

39 triacontakaiennea
40 tetraconta
50 pentaconta
60 hexaconta
70 heptaconta
80 octaconta
90 enneaconta
100 hecta

This should be plenty to keep you naming polyhedra!

positive
A positive integer is a number greater than zero.

power
(See also **base** and **index form**.)
An expression such as 10^4. The expression 10^4 means $10 \times 10 \times 10 \times 10$. 10^4 is the fourth power of 10 and is equal to 10000.

prime factor
A factor of a number such that the factor is also a prime number. For example:

1, 2, 3, 6, 9, 18 are all factors of 18. The numbers 2 and 3 are also prime numbers and hence prime factors of 18.

1, 2, 3, 4, 5, 6, 10, 12 15, 20, 30, 60 are all factors of 60. The numbers 2, 3, 5 are also prime numbers and hence prime factors of 60.

prime number
(See also **Eratosthenes**.)
A whole number that only has factors of 1 and itself. For example, 2, 3, 5, 7, 11, 13

prism
A solid shape with a uniform cross-section. For example:

Rectangular prism

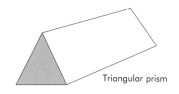

Triangular prism

probability
Used to measure the likelihood of certain events occurring in the future. The probability of an event is always a number between zero and 1.

probability scale
A scale from 0 to 1 that is used to measure the likelihood of an event occurring, with 0 being impossible and 1 being certain.

product
The result of multiplying two or more numbers together. For example, the product of 4×7 is 28.

proper fraction
A fraction in which the numerator is smaller than the denominator, such as $^2/_3$ or $^4/_7$.

property
A feature or characteristic.

proportion
Compares part of a quantity with the whole – for example, a ratio of 1:3 results in proportions of 1 out of 4 and 3 out of 4.

prove
To demonstrate that something will always be so/happen in mathematics. It can involve deductive proof (each step is deduced from the preceding one), proof by exhaustion (finding all possible answers), disproof by counter-example (finding a case that does not match the conjecture), proof by induction (although probably not as relevant for primary schools) and *reductio ad absurdum*. The latter involves reducing something to the absurd, as follows. To prove that it is not possible to divide by zero:

First, assume that it is possible – hence zero behaves like other numbers, e.g. $1 \div 1 = 1$, $37 \div 37 = 1$, $27 \div 27 = 1$, $a \div a = 1$. Hence $0 \div 0 = 1$.

If $2 \times 0 = 3 \times 0 = 0$, dividing by 0 gives:

$$\frac{2 \times 0}{0} = \frac{3 \times 0}{0}$$

Cancelling the zeros gives:

$$\frac{2 \times \cancel{0}^1}{0_1} = \frac{3 \times \cancel{0}^1}{0_1}$$

$\therefore 2 = 3$ (clearly absurd!).

pyramid
A solid that has a polygon base and all the other faces are triangular.

Pythagoras (582–507 BCE)
A Greek philosopher and geometrician. He founded the Pythagorean Brotherhood, a secretive group who refused to share their mathematical discoveries. They believed that all numbers were rational and nearly killed the member who discovered $\sqrt{2}$, an irrational number! Their secretive ways all back-fired rather unpleasantly when, owing to the suspicions and fear of the locals, and encouraged by a rival of Pythagoras, many of the Brotherhood, including their leader, were killed when their buildings were set alight.

Pythagoras' theorem
This theorem states that it is possible to calculate the length of the hypotenuse (longest side) of a right-angled triangle by finding the square root of the sum of the squares of the other two sides. The following diagram illustrates this theorem:

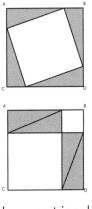

The square in the middle of the four triangles is the square on the hypotenuse of any of these triangles.

The square ABCD remains unchanged. By moving the four triangles it is possible to create two squares instead of one. These two squares are on the other two sides of the triangle. Because the area of ABCD remains unchanged the sum of the areas of the two smaller squares must be equal to the area of the square on the hypotenuse.

In some triangles it is very easy to calculate the length of the hypotenuse as all the numbers are whole numbers – for example, a 3, 4, 5 triangle or a 5, 12, 13 triangle. Sets of three whole numbers that perfectly fit Pythagoras' equation are called Pythagorean triples.

quadrant

Each one of the four sections created as the x and y-axes divide the co-ordinate plane. The quadrants are numbered in an anti-clockwise direction starting in the upper-right quadrant, the first quadrant where both the x and y co-ordinates are positive, and finishing in the bottom-right quadrant, the fourth quadrant where the x co-ordinates are positive and the y co-ordinates are negative.

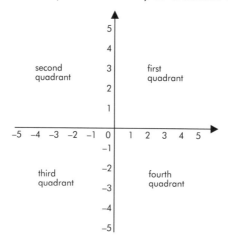

quadrilateral

A four-sided polygon. If it is regular it is called a square:

quotient

The result when one number is divided by another number – for example 6 is the quotient when 24 is divided by 4.

radius

The distance from the centre of a circle to any point on the circumference:

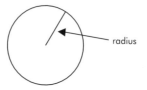

random
Taking a sample from a population so that all members of the population have the same chance of being included.

range
The interval between the greatest and least values in a set of data. For example, in the set of test scores 7, 8, 8, 9, 10, 10, 11, 13, 15, 15, 17, 18 the range is 11 (18−7).

ratio
A comparison between two quantities. It is written as either $a:b$ or as a fraction $^a/_b$, for example, 3:5 or $^3/_5$.

rational number
The set of all numbers that can be written as fractions − for example, ½, 4, $^8/_3$... The set of rational numbers together with the set of irrational numbers gives the set of real numbers. The symbol used to represent the set of irrational numbers is R.

real number
The set of rational numbers and irrational numbers combined. The symbol used to represent the set of real numbers is D.

rectangle
A quadrilateral with four right angles. Each pair of opposite sides is equal in length and parallel. The diagonals are also equal in length and bisect each other. Rectangles have at least two lines of reflective symmetry and rotational symmetry of at least order 2. Why 'at least'? The square fits the general description of a rectangle but has different symmetry properties.

recurring
Decimal fractions that go on for ever are called recurring decimals. Examples include:

$$^1/_3 = 0.3333333...$$
$$^{10}/_{11} = 0.90909090...$$

In order to record that the decimal recurs without having to write it as above dots are used to indicate the cycle of digits that is recurring. The above recurring decimals would be recorded as:

$$^1/_3 = 0.\dot{3} \qquad ^{10}/_{11} = 0.\dot{9}\dot{0}$$

reduced to
To simplify a fraction by dividing by common factors. For example:

$$\frac{4}{8} = \frac{1}{2} \qquad \frac{18}{48} = \frac{3}{8}$$

reduction
Combining different parts of an equation to make it simpler.

reflection
When a shape is reflected a mirror image is created. If the shape and size remain unchanged, the two images are congruent.

reflective symmetry
(Also sometimes called line symmetry.) A shape is said to have reflective symmetry if it can be folded so that one half fits exactly on top of the other half. (See also **axis of symmetry**.)

reflex angle
An angle that is greater than 180° but less than 360°. For example:

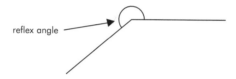

reflex angle

regular
(See also **dihedral angle**.)
A regular polygon has all sides of equal length and all angles of equal size. In a regular polyhedron, all the faces are the same (a regular polygon) – hence all the edges are the same length. The dihedral angles are also all equal.

restoration
Simplifying an equation by performing the same operation on each side.

Rhind papyrus
Named after the Scottish Egyptologist, Alexander Henry Rhind, who acquired it in 1858. It is also sometimes called the 'Ahmes Papyrus' after the scribe who wrote it in about 1650 BCE. He stated that it was copied from an even earlier document of around 2000 BCE. It is now kept in the British Museum. This papyrus contains the first documentary evidence of the use of algebra.

rhombus
A quadrilateral with four sides of equal length. Opposite sides are parallel and opposite angles are equal in size. The

diagonals bisect each other at right angles. A rhombus has at least two lines of reflective symmetry and rotational symmetry of order 2. If the interior angles of the rhombus are equal (i.e. 90°) then it is a square.

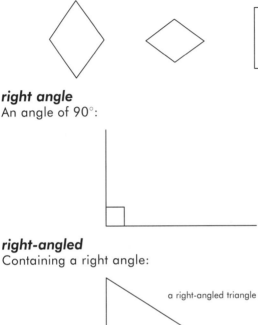

right angle
An angle of 90°:

right-angled
Containing a right angle:

a right-angled triangle

Roman numerals
Seven letters are used in combination to write numbers:

I	=	1
V	=	5
X	=	10
L	=	50
C	=	100
D	=	500
M	=	1000

The system works in the following way. If a letter representing a smaller number appears after a larger number then it is added:

$$XII \quad = \quad 12$$
$$CLXVI \quad = \quad 166$$

If a letter representing a smaller number appears before a larger number then it is subtracted:

$$IX = 9$$
$$XIV = 14$$
$$CXLII = 142$$

rotate

Rotation involves a turn around a fixed point. If the shape and size remain unchanged, the two images are congruent.

rotational symmetry

A shape is said to have rotational symmetry if it looks the same in different positions when rotated about its centre:

(In these diagrams the spot is there to help identify the order of rotational symmetry and should not be considered part of the square.)

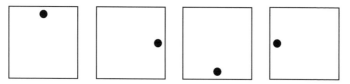

It can be seen that, in each of the four positions above, the square looks exactly the same. So, the order of rotational symmetry of the square is 4. This book is a rectangle. If it is rotated it can be seen that a rectangle has rotational symmetry of order 2. Any shape, however strange, will have rotational symmetry of at least order 1 since there is one position where it looks the same!

rounding

An approximation used to express a number in a more convenient way. Rounding is very useful when estimating an answer. When rounding to the nearest ten, numbers ending in 0, 1, 2, 3, 4 are rounded down, whilst those ending in 5, 6, 7, 8, 9 are rounded up. As can be seen these divide into two equally sized sets of five. This extends so that when considering tenths, 0–4.9 are rounded down and 5–9.9 are rounded up (again two equally sized sets).

row

A horizontal arrangement. For example, a row of numbers:

$$2 \quad 4 \quad 6 \quad 8 \quad 10 \quad 12 \quad 14$$

rule

A mathematical procedure or a definition. It is a definition in cases such as the four 'rules' of number but it is a procedure when considering the order of precedence of operations.

scalene triangle

A triangle which has three sides of different length and no equal angles:

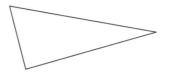

scattergraph

A graph representing two types of data plotted as co-ordinates. It is possible to use a scattergraph to make decisions about correlation between the two sets of data.

sector

This is a wedge from a circle (like a slice of pie!).

segment

A region of a circle bounded by an arc and a chord:

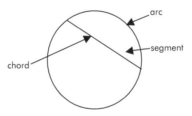

semi-circle

Semi means 'half' – hence a semi-circle is half a circle. The straight edge is the diameter of the circle.

sequence

A set of numbers governed by a particular rule. For example:

$$1, 4, 9, 16, 25, 36$$

The general term for a sequence is n^2.

set

A collection of objects. Each object is called a member of the set. Brackets are used to enclose all the members of the set – for example, $\{w, x, y, z\}$.

side

The straight edge of a polygon.

sieve of Eratosthenes

(See *Eratosthenes*.)

sigma
This means 'the sum of'. The symbol for sigma is Σ.

significant figures
Used in rounding. Instead of rounding to the nearest ten or hundred it is possible to round to a certain number of significant figures. For example the number 26784 can be rounded to 30000 (one significant figure), 27000 (two significant figures) or 26800 (three significant figures). It is rarely appropriate to round to more than three significant figures.

similarity
Shapes are said to be similar if all the angles are the same size and the shapes are the same but of different size (i.e. one is an enlargement of the other).

simultaneous linear equations
Two linear equations which have a common solution. For example, $a - 3b = 1$ and $a + 2b = 11$ have a common solution when $a = 7$ and $b = 2$.

solid
(See also **three-dimensional shape.**)
A three-dimensional shape.

sphere
A solid with a curved surface such that every point on the surface is an equal distance from the centre of the solid:

spiral
A coiled shape in two dimensions.

square
A regular quadrilateral. Because it is regular all four sides are of equal length and all four angles are equal (right angles). The diagonals of a square are equal in length and bisect each other at right angles. It has four lines of reflective symmetry and rotational symmetry of order 4.

square number
A number raised to the second power (i.e. multiplied by itself). Square numbers can be represented pictorially as squares. For example:

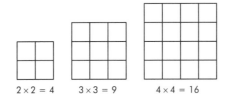

$2 \times 2 = 4$ $3 \times 3 = 9$ $4 \times 4 = 16$

square root
The inverse of a square number. It is a number which, when raised to the second power, gives a particular square number. For example, 6 is the square root of 36 because $6 \times 6 = 36$. Symbolically it is written as $\sqrt{36} = 6$ (the square root of 36 is equal to 6).

standard form
Sometimes called standard index form as it uses powers of 10 (i.e. 10 expressed in index form). It is a shorthand way of writing very small and very large numbers that would require a huge number of digits if written in full, e.g. $6000000 = 6 \times 10^6$.

standard unit
Standard units of measure ensure consistency. When communicating measures standard units ensure the correct mass is given, distance covered, and so on. The first people to use standard units were the Babylonians and Sumerians, who used standard masses made from metal or stone.

statistics
Statistics help us to bring order to data and to draw information from it.

straight angle
An angle of 180°:

subtract
The inverse of addition in which the subtrahend is taken from the minuend.

subtrahend
The number or term to be subtracted.

sum
Another word that means 'add'. Colloquially it is used to mean any of the four operations. However, this is technically not correct.

supplementary angles
(See also **complementary angles**.)
Angles that are adjacent to each other on a straight line (i.e. two angles whose sum is 180°).

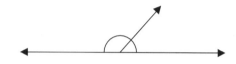

symbol
A letter, numeral or other sort of mark used to represent a number, operation or relationship.

symmetry/symmetrical
(See **reflective symmetry** and **rotational symmetry**.)

Système Internationale (S.I.)
Determines the units of measurement used in the metric system. For each aspect of measurement it specifies one base unit. There are seven different base units, but only three are used within primary school measurement – the kilogram (mass), the metre (length) and the second (time). Other metric units for measures are shown below:

Measure	Unit
Mass	1000 grams (g) = 1 kilogram (kg); 1000 kilograms = 1 tonne
Length	10 millimetres (mm) = 1 centimetre (cm); 100 centimetres = 1 metre (m); 1000 metres = 1 kilometre (km)
Area	100 square millimetres (mm^2) = 1 square centimetre (cm^2); 10 000 square centimetres = 1 square metre (m^2)
Volume	1000 cubic millimetres (mm^3) = 1 cubic centimetre (cm^3); 1 000 000 cubic centimetres = 1 cubic metre (m^3)
Capacity	10 millilitres (ml) = 1 centilitre (cl); 100 centilitres (1000 ml) = 1 litre (l)

table
A method for collecting or representing data.

tally
A base-5 counting record:

Shoe size	Number of children
1	|||
2	̶H̶H̶ |||
3	̶H̶H̶ ̶H̶H̶ ||
4	̶H̶H̶ ||
5	||||
6	||

tangram
An ancient Chinese puzzle first made about 4000 years ago. It consists of a square made out of seven pieces:

terms
Algebraic quantities that are separated from each other in expressions by operations.

tessellation
Shapes fitted together with a number of exact copies and with no overlaps or gaps:

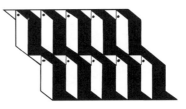

tetrahedron
A polyhedron with four faces. If it is regular it has four equilateral triangles for the faces and is one of the Platonic solids. For example:

T

theoretical probability
The number between 0 and 1 that is found by dividing the number of actual outcomes by the total number of possible outcomes.

three-dimensional shape
(Also written as 3-D or 3D.) A solid shape as opposed to a plane (flat) shape.

transformation
Involves changing a shape in a given way so that every point on the original shape relates to the corresponding point on the new shape in a particular way. Transformations encountered in a primary setting are translations, rotations, reflections and scaling.

transitivity
A mathematical relationship used to compare two objects or events. For example, if A is shorter than B, and B is shorter than C, then A must be shorter than C.

translation
This takes place when a shape is moved from one place to another just by sliding it (without rotating, reflecting or enlarging).

trapezium
A quadrilateral with one pair of parallel sides:

This trapezium is an isosceles trapezium. It has two sides of equal length, base angles of equal size and diagonals which are equal in length.

triangle
A polygon with three sides:

triangle numbers
In the same way that square numbers form squares, triangle numbers form triangles!

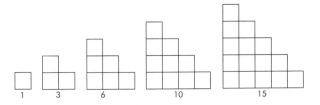

1	3	6	10	15

twin primes

(See **Eratosthenes**.)

Pairs of prime numbers separated by only one other number (an even number) – for example, 11 and 13, 29 and 31.

two-dimensional shape

(Also written as 2-D or 2D.) A plane (flat) shape as opposed to a solid shape.

unique

One, and only one, outcome. For example, when adding two numbers there is only one possible outcome.

unit

The basis of a measurement system.

upper quartile

The value three quarters the way along a set of ordered data.

Venn diagram

Created by John Venn (1834–1923). He was a philosopher and mathematician – a pioneer of logic and probability theory who taught at Gonville and Caius College, Cambridge. A Venn diagram is an illustration of the relationships between and among sets or groups of objects that share something in common. Items are linked by characteristics or attributes. The characteristics items have in common lie in the intersecting portion; and those that differ in the non-intersecting portions:

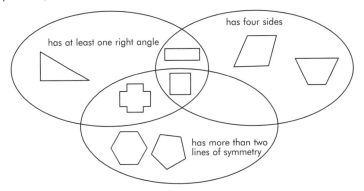

vertex
(Plural, vertices.)
The point of intersection of edges:

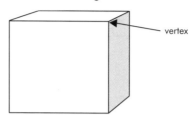

vertical
Perpendicular (i.e. at right angles) to the horizontal plane:

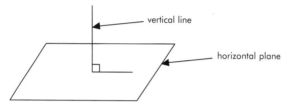

volume
The amount of 3-D space an object occupies. It is measured in cubic units – for example, cm^3.

weight
The force exerted on a body due to gravity. The unit of measure is the newton, named after Sir Isaac Newton.

whole numbers
The set of numbers {0, 1, 2, 3, 4, 5, 6....}. (See also **counting numbers** and **natural numbers**.)

Wiles, Andrew
(See **Fermat, Pierre de**.)

x-axis
Axes are lines used to locate points on graphs. The horizontal number line is called the x-axis. **Cartesian co-ordinates** use the distance along the x-axis and the distance along the y-axis to locate a point:

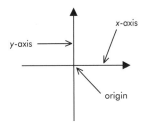

y-axis

Axes are lines used to locate points on graphs. The vertical number line is called the y-axis. **Cartesian co-ordinates** use the distance along the x-axis and the distance along the y-axis to locate a point.

y-intercept

The point at which a graph crosses the y-axis. In the following graph it can be seen that the graph crosses the y-axis at the point (0, 2) – i.e. when y = 2. This point is the y-intercept:

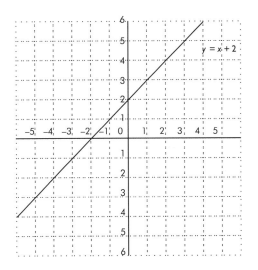

zero

Comes from the Latin *zephirum*, which means empty or blank. It is used to symbolise the empty set (i.e. a set containing no elements) – for example, the set of people living in the world who are over 5 metres tall! It is also used as a 'place holder' in our place value number system. The role of 0 as a place holder is crucial. When 2 is multiplied by 10, the answer is 20. The zero is holding the place for the units (ones) to show that the units (ones) column is empty. The symbol 0 originated in India. Al-Khwarizmi explained the Indian number system in 830, but it took a further 400 years before zero was used in western number systems.

Useful Resources

The following is a list of some possible resources for a primary classroom – but it is by no means definitive or exhaustive!

- abacus
- angle measurer
- arrow cards/place value cards
- balance
- cog clocks
- compare bears
- compasses
- counters
- Cuisenaire rods
- die/dice
- digit cards
- geo-strips
- hundred square
- masses
- measuring cylinder
- metre stick
- multilink cubes
- number grid
- number line
- number square
- number track
- peg board
- pin board
- plane shapes
- protractor
- scales
- set square
- solid shapes
- spinner
- tape measure
- timers

Publications for teachers

Askew, M. and Selinger, M. (1998) *Teaching Primary Mathematics: A Guide for Newly Qualified and Student Teachers.* London: Hodder & Stoughton Educational. A pre-National Numeracy Strategy book that aims to support trainees and NQTs get to grips with National Curriculum mathematics at Key Stages 1 and 2. It contains a selection of activities and resources to help teachers develop strategies for each of the four mathematics curriculum areas. Case studies are used to exemplify examples of teaching and learning mathematics. It also exemplifies cross-curricular links to other subjects and topics.

Brown, T. (1998) *Coordinating Mathematics Across the Primary School.* London: Falmer Press. Another pre-NNS book that considers issues associated with coordinating the mathematics curriculum within schools. For those training as mathematics specialists or those having to coordinate maths for the first time it is a useful source book. Although the NNS has been introduced into many schools in England, many of the issues related to coordinating mathematics are still very current.

DfEE (1999a) *The National Numeracy Strategy: framework for teaching mathematics.* London: DfEE.

DfEE (1999b) *The National Numeracy Strategy: mathematical vocabulary.* London: DfEE.

DfEE/QCA (1999) *Mathematics: the National Curriculum for England.* London: HMSO.

Frobisher et al (1999) *Learning to Teach Number in the Primary School: A Handbook for Students and Teachers.* Cheltenham: Nelson Thornes. This book is written for primary trainees. It aims to provide an overview of the key issues in a range of mathematical areas with useful suggestions for class activities.

Haylock, D. (2001) *Mathematics Explained for Primary Teachers.* London: Paul Chapman Publishing. As the title suggests, this book explains much of the content of the primary mathematics curriculum. It also addresses key teaching points and gives opportunities to try some self-assessment questions in each area.

Mooney, C. and Fletcher, M. (2003) *Primary mathematics: audit and test (2nd edn).* Exeter: Learning Matters.

Mooney, C., Ferrie, L., Fox, S., Hansen, A. and Wrathmell, R. (2002a) *Primary mathematics: knowledge and understanding (2nd edn).* Exeter: Learning Matters. This book addresses the subject knowledge requirements for primary mathematics as set out in the Professional Standards for QTS, making clear links with the pupils' National Curriculum and with the NNS.

Mooney, C., Briggs, M., Fletcher, M. and McCullouch, H. (2002b) *Primary mathematics: teaching theory and practice (2nd edn).* Exeter: Learning Matters. An invaluable guide to primary mathematics teaching, which includes case studies of classroom situations to help trainees make the link between teaching theory and classroom practice.

Orton and Frobisher (2002) *Insights into Teaching Maths.* London: Continuum International Publishing Group. A book offering a balance between the theory and practice of teaching mathematics. It offers analysis and evaluation of mathematics teaching contextualised within recent developments.

QCA (1999a) *Standards in mathematics: exemplification of key learning objectives from reception to year 6*. London: QCA.

QCA (1999b) *The National Numeracy Strategy: teaching mental calculation strategies – guidance for teachers at Key Stages 1 and 2*. London QCA.

QCA (2000) *Curriculum guidance for the Foundation Stage*. London: QCA.

Thompson, I. (ed.) (1999) *Issues in Teaching Numeracy in Primary Schools*. Buckingham: Open University Press. This book covers many of the issues of current concern associated with developing numeracy in primary schools, including studies of effective teacher numeracy and ICT and numeracy, an evaluation of international primary textbooks, assessment, using and applying mathematics, and family numeracy. The book also includes chapters on pedagogy, focusing on the teaching of mental calculation, the transition from mental to written algorithms, the place of the empty number line, and the use of the calculator as a teaching aid.

Thompson, I. (ed.) (1997) *Teaching and Learning Early Number*. Buckingham: Open University Press. This is an accessible book detailing current research into the teaching and learning of early number concepts. The beliefs and number understanding of Nursery and Reception children are considered, alongside a detailed summary of the role of counting in the acquisition of number understanding.

TTA (2002) *Qualifying to Teach: Professional Standards for the Award of Qualified Teacher Status and Requirements for Initial Teacher Training*. London: TTA.

Williams, E. and Shuard, H. (1994) *Primary Mathematics Today*. London: Longman. A pre-NNS book, this is a detailed, yet still accessible book containing a great deal of information about the development of mathematical understanding throughout the primary years. One of the most comprehensive books written about primary mathematics, which is still very relevant today.

Publications – popular maths

Many 'popular' mathematics books have been written, with a significant number being published in recent years. These books do a great deal to promote mathematics within society and make explicit the role of mathematics in so many aspects of our culture. Some books consider very specific aspects of mathematics (see *To Infinity and Beyond*, *E: the Story of a Number* and *E=mc^2* below); others consider some of the people involved (see *Fermat's Last Theorem* and *A Mathematician's Apology*); others use mathematics as the stimulus for a novel (*Uncle Petros and Goldbach's Conjecture*); whilst others look more broadly at aspects of mathematics (*The Magical Maze, The Mathematical Universe* and *The Penguin Dictionary of Curious and Interesting Numbers*). The following books offer an introduction to the different types currently available, which popularise mathematics, are easy to read, and are most definitely not 'heavy' mathematical tomes – enjoy!

Bodanis, D. (2001) $E=mc^2$: *A Biography of the World's Most Famous Equation*. London: Pan.

Doxiadis, A. (2001) *Uncle Petros and Goldbach's Conjecture*. London: Faber and Faber.

Dunham, W. (1997) *The Mathematical Universe: An Alphabetical Journey Through the Great Proofs, Problems, and Personalities*. Chichester: John Wiley & Sons Inc.

Hardy, G. H. (1992) *A Mathematician's Apology (CANTO)*. Cambridge: Cambridge University Press.

Maor, E. (1998) *E: the Story of a Number*. New Jersey: Princeton University Press.

Maor, E. (1991) *To Infinity and Beyond: A Cultural History of the Infinite*. New Jersey, Princeton University Press.

Singh, S. (2002) *Fermat's Last Theorem*. London: Fourth Estate.

Stewart, I. (1998) *The Magical Maze: Seeing the World Through Mathematical Eyes*. London: Phoenix.

Wells, D. (1997) *The Penguin Dictionary of Curious and Interesting Numbers*. London: Penguin Books.

Useful websites

The Standards Site (**www.standards.dfee.gov.uk/numeracy**) – download useful resources from the NNS and keep up-to-date with current initiatives.

The DfES home page (**www.dfes.gov.uk/index.htm**) – keep up to date with the latest education publications from the government.

The TTA home page (**www.canteach.gov.uk**) – useful links to the Professional Standards and the Career Entry Profile.

The QCA home page (**www.qca.org.uk/**) – from here link to the mathematics National Curriculum online as well as other useful mathematics resources.

NRICH (the on-line maths club) (**nrich.maths.org/index.html**) – a great sources of ideas, games, puzzles, resources, news and articles.

Ask dr math (**www.askdrmath.com**) – a useful site to help find the answer to all those mathematical questions you might have.

The online mathematical dictionary from Intermath – **www.intermath-uga.gatech.edu/dictionary/**

The BEAM (BE A Mathematician) home page (**www.beam.co.uk/**) – a great place to order really useful resources for supporting your teaching of mathematics.

The Association of Teachers of Mathematics home page (**www.atm.org.uk/**) – a professional organisation to join producing regular journals and useful resources for supporting the teaching of mathematics.

The Mathematical Association home page (**www.m-a.org.uk/**) – another professional organisation to support the teaching and learning of mathematics.

Useful resources

As ICT is such a dynamic area specific packages or CD-Roms identified here are likely to be superseded by something else very soon. However there are certain packages that are updated regularly and are very useful in schools:

Logo – available in a range of versions for both Key Stage 1 and Key Stage 2, it is a simple programming language and is very useful for developing geometric understanding.

Pinpoint – again regularly updated and available in formats suitable for both Key Stage 1 and Key Stage 2, a really useful data handling package.

My World – new screens are frequently added and the programme is regularly updated. Very appropriate for use with children from the Foundation Stage upwards for a range of mathematical activities.

Crystal Rainforest – a Key Stage 2 adventure into maths and Logo. The adventure context makes this extremely popular in the classroom.

Certain companies produce a range of mathematics software for use in schools. Some of these are listed below:

The Association of Teachers of Mathematics **www.atm.org.uk**
Granada Learning **www.granada-learning.com/school/**
Logotron Educational Software **www.logotron.co.uk**
Sherston Software Limited **www.sherston.com**
Topologika Software **www.topologika.co.uk**

Appendix

mathematical symbols

+   add
−   subtract
±   plus or minus
×   multiply
÷   divide
√   square root
=   equals
≈   is approximately equal to
≅   is congruent to (in shapes)
<   is less than
>   is greater than
⩾   is greater than or equal to
≤   is less than or equal to
%   percentage
°   degrees
∞   infinity
∴   therefore

large numbers

(See also **google/googleplex**.)

These numbers are all powers of ten. The number names recorded here represent the American system which is in common usage throughout the mathematics community. In each number it is assumed there is a 1 in the column preceding all the columns containing zero:

number of zeros	number name	
3	thousand	(1 000)
6	million	(1 000 000)
9	billion	(1 000 000 000)
12	trillion	(and so on)
15	quadrillion	
18	quintillion	
21	sextillion	
24	septillion	
27	octillion	
30	nonillion	
33	decillion	
36	undecillion	
39	duodecillion	
42	tredecillion	
45	quattuordecillion	
48	quindecillion	

51	sexdecillion
54	septendecillion
57	octodecillion
60	novemdecillion

prefixes

mega (M)	×	1 000 000
kilo (k)	×	1 000
hecto (h)	×	100
deca (da)	×	10
deci (d)	×	0.1
centi (c)	×	0.01
milli (m)	×	0.001
micro (μ)	×	0.000001